These poems—at times grim and violent, tender
and compassionate—bristle with a necessary and
defiant anger at the violence men and their institutions
wreak upon women. They also narrate a singular
woman's journey through the serial hells of male
violence and governmental indifference. In these
poems Jancis Andrews sings the song of the abused
woman and her achievement of a difficult survival
and grace. A necessary work.

—Pierre Coupey

In her *Ballad*, Mr Smith teaches his Missus how home
is a river that runs red with the blood from her nose,
her ears. And from the bright light of his white fist, she
learns to see how the other half lives when cast out of
Vancouver's ritzy British Properties into the Downtown
Eastside. With tender and relentless eye she picks up
its discarded butts, like the neighbours and herself,
"dying by inches," and its beauties: grandmothers in
Chinatown, "clasping grandchildren, small sprigs of
cherry blossom"; or the copulating rapture of two slugs
"inscribed in silver" in Oppenheimer Park. The corners
of Mrs Smith's mouth and these verses brim with bitter

and bawdy humour, subtle as thyme and cyanide, coarse and dark as Demerara sugar. Her *Ballad* does in poetry what *Diary of a Mad Housewife* could never do in prose. Only Jancis Andrews' poetry could inscribe Mrs Smith's story on our senses and brand it indelibly on any posh sensitivities we have for the destitute descended into the unholies of East Hastings Street. Through the dialogues with Joe, Peaches, Rose, the *Ballad* follows how abuse blossoms into scarred charismatic character, odorous oddballs and philosh-ophers. Now, when blood runs on the Downtown Eastside, Mrs Smith has learned her lesson, she knows what to do: "semi-good Samaritan," she phones Vancouver General and "like a screaming angel, an ambulance touches down." Like this book, bringing care—for and to the wounded.

—*George McWhirter*

The Ballad of Mrs Smith

The Ballad of Mrs Smith

JANCIS M. ANDREWS

HEDGEROW PRESS

Some of these poems first appeared in the following
periodicals: *Boa, Canadian Dimension, Canadian Woman
Studies, Carnegie Newsletter, Cokefish, The Fisherman,
Mr. Cogito, One Page, Portraits, The Vancouver Sun,
Verve, Women's Education Des Femmes*, and in the
anthologies *Living the Edges, A Verse Map of Vancouver,
Walk Myself Home.*

Library and Archives Canada Cataloguing in Publication
Andrews, Jancis M. (Jancis Maureen), 1934–
    The Ballad of Mrs Smith / Jancis M. Andrews
Poems.

ISBN 978-1-926618-01-2
1. Abused women — Poetry. 2. Downtown-Eastside
(Vancouver, B.C.) — Poetry. I. Title.
PS8551.N372B36 2012   C811'.54   C2012-902146-6

Published by
Hedgerow Press
Box 2471
Sidney, B.C. V8L 3Y3
hedgep@telus.net
www.hedgerowpress.com

Cover and text design: Frances Hunter
The cover art is from the painting "Ongoing" (oil and acrylic)
by Carolyn Bell, from the collection of Marian Brant.

Printed and bound in Canada

CONTENTS

Mr and Mrs Smith Have One of Their Little Chats   11

Mrs S. Talks to the Marriage Counsellor   12

Extra-Rich Dessert   13

Bloodlines   14

Ill Wind   16

Sleeping Out   17

East Hastings   18

Rooming House   19

Roomers   20

Meeting the Neighbours or Civilization is Only Ten Thousand Years Old   21

Bathroom Meeting   23

Old Olaf (Room 2)   24

Mrs Malinowski (Room 3)   25

Old Joe (Room 6)   26

Asking for Directions to the Job Centre   27

Job Opportunity   28

Falling Off the Wagon   30

Grandmothers in Chinatown   31

Second Job Attempt   32

Slow Dancing in Oppenheimer Park   34

Mrs S. Talks About her Childhood in Northumbria, England   35

Balancing Act   37

Rose's File   38

Free Breakfast on the Sunday before Welfare Wednesday   39

Mrs S.'s Conception   40

La Quena Coffeehouse   41

To the Cockroach Fallen in Her Cereal Bowl   42

Little Lessons   43

Peaches Talks About Her Mother   45

And Then About Her Father   46

Gastown   48

On Being Ordered to Cover Her Hair   49

Lest We Forget 51

Deconsecrated
    Church 52

Deaf Mute? 53

Pay-Off 54

Dr Mario 55

Mrs S. Finds a
    Broken Christmas
    Ornament During
    the "Access for the
    Handicapped"
    Protest, Crab Park 56

Second Service at
    First United
    Church 58

Carnegie Centre 59

Mrs S. Walks
    Around Her Wine
    Bottle 60

Drunk On Main
    Street 61

Wordbound in the
    Carnegie Learning
    Centre 63

Birthday Party on
    Crab Park Beach 64

Ash City (Watching
    the Film, *The Blue
    Angel*) 65

Final Trip 66

Prostitutes Outside
    First United
    Church 67

Welfare Wednesday 68

The Abandoned Cat 69

Peaches, Rose and
    Mrs S. Take Tea 70

Homing 71

Murder is the
    World's Oldest
    Profession 72

In Memoriam 74

Mrs S. Talks to
    the Divorce
    Lawyer 75

Epiphany in
    Oppenheimer
    Park 77

Ann Jones
    (ex-Mrs S.)
    Learns She Has
    a Brain Tumour 78

Acceptance 81

Mr and Mrs Smith Have One of Their
Little Chats

He: I need a grid
to find out where you are. Bearing a cross
reference of letter to number
I might strike
lucky—pinpoint even you
on your complicated map, riddled
with diversions and dead ends.
God knows I need some sort of tool
to straighten the paths
of your convoluted thinking, re-work
this tattered map into a tapestry.
But what's the use! You're no embroidery
needle, only your own one-eyed, pie-eyed
erratic compass, and let me tell you, Mrs S.,
in this journey, getting there
sure isn't half the fun.

She: If I am the eye of a needle,
you are its coarse
twist dragging me down.
If I am the eye of a needle,
you are its barb
shafting me.
If I am the eye of a needle
you are its steel
hemming me in…
of course, that could mean we two
might finally achieve some sort of harmony—
me, pulling us up and putting us down,
you, tying us in knots—
the two of us stabbing
stitches that pretend to hold
this marriage together.

Mrs S. Talks to the Marriage Counsellor

"Welcome to Knackers Yard, a.k.a.
the Smith residence, British Properties.*
Sit here, where the wind
can blow through your bones
and you can tell me All The Latest
and What This Year Will Be Wearing.
Oh deary me, your expression implies
I carry the Black Death.
Not to worry! I carry my death
in this tall glass…in this delicious non-nutrient
I watch death's roots growing.

By the way, no need to tell me
after the earthquake of a child's death
all landmarks shatter into history,
and husband and wife
lose each other in the rubble.
Teach your granny, eh?

Care to see Mr Smith's excuses?
I frame them and hang them on the wall,
discuss them with each social worker.
Examine those lines! Their cut and thrust!

When you leave, which will be any second now,
why don't you take his character with you?
Without weight, slippery as artificial silk
it might prove useful for bolstering something
in some woman's bedroom,
provided, of course,
that she's not particular."

*An exclusive residential neighbourhood of West Vancouver

Extra-Rich Dessert

A carpenter ant has climbed her kitchen counter
eager to whoop it up with her grasshopper pie.
Such a glittering, ebony body! Such a big, black
helmeted head! Darth Vader
on six hydropole legs!
Mrs S. truly regrets having to kill him
in order to discourage his relatives.
But in death she gives him
what she denied in life
and, for his final resting place, tucks him
into the dark chocolate crumb crust
which soon she will serve
to Mr Smith's latest
who asked down her nose,
"My dear, whatever do you housewives do
to amuse yourselves
all day long?"

Bloodlines

The blood
　is a river the river's
　　a place that's for　drowning　she drowns
　in the blood
from her nose　　from her
　　mouth　　ears
　he says he loved her　　blood
　runs from
the earth from
　　the sky　　love
　is a fist shining
　　　white in the sunlight
　love is a fist and a　boot and a
　　river of　blood
　he says he loved her　it's her fault
　　"It's your fault"
she made him do it　the world burns
　　　blue black it's a
　　　　bruise
　it's her nose　her eyes
he's head of the household a man's home
　is his castle
the Head of the Household
　　　is home and must prove he's
　　　　a man
　he'll prove he's a man
on her nose on her eyes
on her breasts on her chin the Master
　Master　Master　Master
　is King of the Castle
　his white fists prove he's a man
He says he will show her
　　　　　　what's what
　　　he will teach her

the world is a fist it is   God
God shines white
          in the sunlight his heaven is blue
black
    the blood's
  in her nose   mouth
          ears   eyes   God
    proves he's a man
  home in his heaven   Mr Smith teaches
        home
is a river   the river
      runs red
          the river's a place that's for
                drowning

Ill Wind

The coldest day for eighty years, and this wind
lamenting down Carrall Street perfects
the picture where CFRO now sings
the Downtown Eastside blues.
Here too the prostitutes, unemployed
and unemployable,
are buffeted by cries—
doing the Downtown Eastside shuffle
in the crack that opens
between the Sally Bash and the dole run out.
Is it only Mrs S. (two crammed suitcases,
two black eyes, a broken nose,
a missing front tooth)
who notices the wind blowing a newspaper
from its rack, pages lifting
like the skirts of whores, revealing
corporate bum,
the tart—
ing up of business expenses
and the screwing
of the taxpayer?

Sleeping Out

In the underground garage
Mrs S. sleeps
in a cardboard box, as if indicating
her own world has ground to a halt
in this place where cars proclaim
another world that's going somewhere.
Caught up by headlights
she hangs from her own high beam
of catatonia: the black light
that swallows the flash
and lash of tongue of those
who claim they've already paid
one loony
for this six feet of earth.
Welfare recipients
must have a permanent address,
a place to park themselves, and maybe
that's what has drawn her here
to create a box number
of cardboard and neon and a harsh wind
that does not slow down
but hits hard
as the attendant ordering her out.
But she remains motionless, too far gone
into herself, stalled
by her individual defeats
and curled fetus-like
against a human race that careens by
on a southward or a northward
an eastward or a westward exodus,
leaving her behind, packed up
and abandoned in a corner:
an inconvenient parcel
left for someone else to find.

East Hastings

It's 6:00 a.m. and East Hastings
butchers the dreams
of Downtown Eastsiders, nerves ground
to hamburger
by the morning rush.
Horns blare the hours, truck
a rush and clash of insults, soup up
stinks of gasoline.

A prolonged drought
wastes Mrs S.
She is a drained stare
pushing her life in a shopping cart
while the dead child's voice
calls from distance to distance.
Maybe these streets
will scrape her memories clean
leave them to whiten.

Noon will find her still wired
to the white noise in her head
while a metallic sun,
accelerating through the acids of this air,
burns up East Hastings
with two thousand vehicles an hour.

Rooming House

The social worker says Room 4
is hers: a squirrel's nest
where she can hoard each day, let go
confusion. In this small room
she may find the answer that shimmers
always at her fingertips, the message
perhaps hidden in the fall of gold
from Oppenheimer Park, come autumn,
or maybe held there now
in the park's fresh green fingers.
Here is a bed, a chest of drawers, a chair,
the simple furniture
of the mind as it was before
grief and booze
waged war and won.
But these clean thin drapes
raise blue translucent lids
on hope. From this window
she can contemplate tracts
of sun or stars, watch the wind
open white wings among the clouds
anticipate the bridal night
of mind and memory, knowing
she now has somewhere
she can call home.

Roomers

Most roomers here are men, so old
even they have forgotten
the wives and confusion of children
who could wait no longer and went
faces fading, dream flaking
to an ache,
leaving them in this dominion of cockroaches
holding muttered conversations
with stained walls.

Yet even now an intermittent flame
of who they were once
can cross the milky ground of their eyes
like a signature blazed
across the last, blank page
as a book closes
and sometimes one of them lifts a hand
and wonderingly contemplates it
as if the veins rising under his skin
are blue angels come to deliver him
from his interminable twilight.

Meeting the Neighbours
or
Civilization is Only Ten Thousand Years Old

"Peaches" (room 5, daughter Lynn in foster care) reveals
a negligéed leg, presents
peach pie, solicits
the cost of bacon. Mrs S. listens, amazed
streetwalkers do not speak in tongues,
have normal flesh.
"Buy by the bone," Mrs S. advises,
"It's cheaper." A slice
of Peaches' bacon costs thirty bucks, the full bone,
one hundred.
Peaches nibbles a nail, disconcerts
by resembling anybody's daughter, yawns,
and Mrs S. recoils before her tongue, pink
as a worm, pink
as the cocks Peaches cleans off nightly.
Carefully, Mrs S. memorizes the cup
that Peaches drinks from.
"How can you?" Mrs S. asks,
force-feeding herself peach pie,
"*How can you*
get your pastry so light?"
"It's the touch," Peaches says, and is concerned
when Mrs S. chokes.
The girl's hands terrify
with where they've been. This is why,
thinks Mrs S., "decent women"
never will forgive her. Prostitutes
put a match to your fairy tales
and your *Miss Manners*
before opening their own black book to show
Prince Charming urinating on Cinderella,

your daddy grinning
while opening his fly.

Mrs S. can give Peaches thirty years.
Peaches gives Mrs S. ten thousand.

Bathroom Meeting

"Rose" (Peaches' room-mate) is searching for her roots,
the peroxided toothbrush
translating darkness into light.
Mrs S. knows streetwalkers
die young, die in alleys or
inside their heads.
Rose, she guesses, recognizes clients
not by their faces but by their cock
and bull stories of frigid wives and
the stress of business, regards herself
as a public benefactor.
And why not? thinks Mrs S., joining the line-up
for the lavatory:
in Rose's syphilitic country
her vagina is a United Nations, where Black
meets White, and Conservative mingles
with NDP, the sales rep
with his recalcitrant boss.

Old Olaf (Room 2)

A broken bottle's cap flares from the gutter
but signals only a white light.
It's red and black he fears
the nightmares red
in tooth and claw, that want more
than a pound of flesh, and the tumour's black
crab that never sleeps, pincers
thrusting red hot iron in his belly, beating
his days to a red sleep of morphine
his nights
to a wake of black blood.

Grinning at Mrs S.,
he stoops and scoops
a prize:
his life reflected
in a red eye in the dust
the discarded butt, like him,
dying by inches.

Mrs Malinowski (Room 3)

Iva Malinowski (née Dmitrovic)
left school in Grade Four
worked as a washerwoman
in a stone wash house, back bent
over tubs of other people's dirt,
hooking up sheets and shirts with a stick
wrestling them through a wringer, while steam
and her sweat salted
the walls. Then she'd escape
outside, peg up the linen and let it sweeten
in the sun.

When she was sixteen
and barely able to sign her name, a man promised
he'd take her away from all that
and she married and came to Canada
and had eight kids, meaning
she was still a washerwoman.
When she reads a newspaper, she bends
over pages boiling with other people's dirt,
her forefinger labouring under each word
as if to hook it up, her lips wringing out
syllables of rapes, wars and recessions,
pinning up the words
until she gets them right,
her smile radiant, as if she still believes
sunshine and fresh air
cannot fail to sweeten
anything that has been fouled.

Old Joe (Room 6)

Guiseppe (Old Joe, the ex-clerk)
sits in Pigeon Park
subtracting mouthfuls from a hotdog and calculating
the beady arithmetic
of eyes tabulating each crumb. But soon
one pigeon bows around Joe's bunions, followed
by sisters, brothers, cousins, aunts,
uncles, parents, grandparents,
the whole damn familiar lot
throaty with the same complaints
and hard luck stories.
He rings up a finger
swiped across his nose
at those, at these
indefatigable expectants, who pursue
(like them) from place to place,
until he yells, "Andate tutti a fanculo!" *
and tears off another handout, another
ounce of flesh.

*"Go fuck yourselves!"

The drunk stammering his pain
to the wind
could do worse—
he could try Social Services—but for now,
educating yet more empty air
he flails his arms,
perhaps indicating
the north, south, east and west
of his existence spinning yet again
beyond his reach.
His eyes are red-rimmed, burnt earth
of all his hopes, failed fields
yielding nothing but an exhausted answer.
Yet he is fellow-traveller, his mumbling
goes arm-in-arm with hers, the same indecipherable
question without answer, the same incoherent anger
at a world bent
on proving black is white. Mrs S. retreats.
She can always pay him
off with a dollar, herself
she cannot compensate.

Job Opportunity

The women wear white: madonnas
of the morning shift
on minimum wage
they clock in at 6:00 a.m.,
the stilettos that bestow grace
glittering in their hands.

The first truckload arrives:
wicker highrise of white feathers
and boot-button eyes.
The stiletto plunges—crimson star exploding
wings rushing up in one last, mad flight,
fleeing breathless to Paradise
upside-down on hooks.
The room smokes with feathers and blood and
who did what to whom last night.
Blood drenches the coveralls, the women natter,
wade through rank snowdrifts, their hands blooming
with small hearts for the bins.

All day the constellation revolves on its chain
and Heaven hangs on a hook of steel.
The trucks ply to and fro, the women gab
about shopping, stilettos sing
to the gasping angels
the radio plays rhythm and blues
the women keeping time, lightning in their hands:
with a *one* and a *two* and a *three* and a *four*.

By 6:00 p.m. all the white angels
are pink-fleshed and unseeing, and the women
are crimson, their hair leaking feathers,
rushing to an upside-down house
to squawk at latch-key children

and husbands skewered
by bills.

Mrs S. takes ten minutes
to scrub her hands, and two seconds
to tell the foreman
"Thanks for the opportunity,
but no thanks."

Falling Off the Wagon

This fog insinuates
facelessness
everywhere.

It is unreadable:
blurred syllables
brim through grey teeth, slide
over the rooftops.

A telephone pole
floats its crucifix.
Voices
nailed to its drowning arms
whisper,
"Help. Help."

Mrs S. ripples forward
and sinks.
She has swallowed alcohol enough
to blear her edges
her horizons now divided by trees
hanging in the air
unreachable.

And though she cries
and cries
there is no answer.
Her voice passes through Social Services
which opens
and closes
behind it.

Grandmothers in Chinatown

They seem boneless, these women, twigs
of black pants and dragon-embroidered jacket, shuffling
between family and franchise
in a culture still alien
after fifty years.
Their jet eyes reveal nothing
to Mrs S. except an onyx patience: apology—
or intuition maybe—for living.
Stung by her Wasp eye, they twitch
their gaze to oriental jungles
of shark fins, birds' nests, clasping
grandchildren, small sprigs of cherry blossom,
by the hand.

She thinks
what do they have to teach me—the boozy
white-skinned giant
from British Properties—now crashing the barrier
of Chinatown's East Pender Street?
What do I know of dragons, however silken,
that stalk their sleep?
How can I enter a language
shaped like twigs
even though those twigs
be cherry blossom?

Second Job Attempt

Only those white clouds are free
to soar beyond the factory window.
Inside, grey dust scales
the cutter hacking out shirts,
flinging dismembered parts, inanimate
as dead dreams, into open boxes.
Here, life is taped, ruled
"At the double!"…a double seam
yoking body to arm, the double load
of outside job plus housework, the double talk
of a radio playing "Workers' Playtime"
while women sweat for a minimum wage.
Their hands cling to a Singer
racing like a small, frantic beast
towards 5:00 p.m. and freedom
of a sort: life buttoned down
from eight till five, for fifty weeks a year
the stop-and-start
embrace of these whose limp arms hold
only the bone and flesh
of a five-day week plus compulsory overtime.
Their eternal home is this dead end
where Saint Mary is a supervisor
with hennaed hair, steel eyeglasses
and a tongue whipping them forward
and God is a boss
slashing seams and wages.
Neither the singer nor the song
these women
are the reinforcement
between the dole and the rent
due Friday next.
And the young girls marry arm to body,
try to pin life down by the tail

and dream of collaring
a husband, rattling out
short and long stitches: hopeful S.O.S
to that future prince
who will take them away from all this
into a fairy world of wifeydom
where life will be a seamless wonder
and the inside will be as perfect
as the outside.

And the older workers, wiser, turn away,
knowing that in their women's world
all hope hangs only by a thread
and they fold the shirts and entomb
them tight in plastic, seeing
in these pale look-alikes
an image of themselves
boxed in, straight-jacketed
in cut-rate, throw-away packages.

Slow Dancing in Oppenheimer Park

Two green slugs copulate, slow-dancing
re-creation, luminous trails
blazed on soft flesh
in a spell wrought
by these trees' breathing silence.
Bride and bridegroom
of sensuousness and slow earth
their dim ecstasy dissolves
in soft, exploratory caress
as they seek to root
one in the other.
Mrs S. asks herself
who would not envy
their timeless caress
and silent delight?
Never having been banished
from Eden, they are free
of the morning aftermaths
of regrets, recriminations,
compulsory clock-watching, the black death
of performance pressures
and the rising decibels
of love's disillusion.
This unhurried moment is all,
as their obscure universe turns
as it should, their rapture
inscribed in silver
in this ferny stillness
of seed pods and spider webs starred
with night rain, their pavane
to the sun's measure.

Mrs S. Talks About her Childhood in Northumbria, England

I celebrate women's work, the work
of my foremothers, the beauty
of the weekly wash defying skies grey
with slag heaps and poverty and lives
held cheap, in winds pockmarked
with coal dust and sour with gasometers
and black lung. I celebrate
muscle and sweat
scourging tablecloths and tea towels
in a grimy rainbow of suds and black grit,
the Monday baptisms
in the battered washtubs and outside cold water taps
of miners' row housing. I celebrate
the white flames of washing
lighting dark back alleys, the triumphal banners
of pillowslips and bath towels greeting
husbands condemned to the pit
and choking on coal dust, only the whites
of their eyes
signalling the end of each shift
as the years clock in and clock out
with the blind pit ponies dragging coal.

Oh, invincible women! Salt of the earth
scouring the centuries,
doing battle day in and day out
girded only in an apron, your weapons
bent backs and a hard yellow soap
and harder water,
standing soaked through and immoveable
in slum backyards, up to your armpits
in steam and the rhythms of washing
wringing out dirt as if it were the neck

of the enemy, your hands red and raw
as your lives; gasping and victorious as each sheet
rises like a miracle above soot-blackened streets,
rises like a great white heron loosed to the heavens
on majestically flapping, wet, pristine wings
in the white dance of women, white ceremony
of washday, the sweet-smelling
spotless testaments to love.

Balancing Act

The johns are cruising in their diseases
and here's ex-neighbour Mr McFee, Chief Accountant,
eager to sacrifice new shoes for his kids
on the altar
of this red light.
Streets make a double entry
on children who haggle
before being fucked by What's-His-Name
from British Properties or West Point Grey.
Mrs S. watches McFee comparison shop
and sashays up to purr,
"The kids on Georgia will blow your horn
for one hundred bucks,
the economy models on Pender
make a man of you for thirty,
but—caveat emptor!—
no matter how carefully you estimate
you can still be called to account
in God's little acre
aided
by Adam's worm."

Rose's File

Whining his excuses,
her father prowled the small hours.
An impersonal lust had invoked his daughter.
Rose woke to the red eye in the dark,
her frail frontiers ravaged
by a recurring nightmare: his hands
invading like a marauding army, his penis
forcing its savage history in her mouth,
afterwards, wearing Rose
like a small, split flower.

Thus rent, Rose was forced to divide,
her mind fleeing to a terra intacta
of teddy bears, dolls, a Noddy-Nodkins land
where daddies are not allowed
and elves take her hands,
fly her to the protected side of the moon,
her body left behind, pinioned to a dread
where Mommy turned resolute eyes
from the claw that comes in the night
the deaths
that must be lived
over and over.

*Free Breakfast on the Sunday before
Welfare Wednesday** *

The porridge pot has fed seventy,
and on the stove an extra pot
rises to a slow boil.
But a dozen men are waiting, anxiety
rising, gaze dividing porridge
by serving spoon and guesstimating
six men shall eat
and six men shall not.
And here is the thin skin
of white heat simmering
on a famine
of government help, the slow boil
that might explode,
burn down the house,
taking our world with it, maybe cauterizing
their own world's wounds,
when six men without food—only the ash
of defeat in their mouths—
consume the faces
of seventy-six who eat, eyes averted,
in this church hall where hope
goes up in smoke, this breakfast
that does not break their fast
only breaks us all.

*Welfare cheques are paid on the first Wednesday of every month.

Mrs S.'s Conception

I was not conceived on a stained mattress
behind chipped paint in one of the pit houses.
My house was a flowered field, its roof shingled
with stars.

Housemaid and miner
missing the last bus on a crystalline night,
one beer too many, a moonlit glaze on the grass,
small night birds lyrical in a shadowy tree.
Mother still in her dream from the picture house,
Father an underground Clark Gable
in his coal-black hair.
I was languishing in line
and the moon lifted me forward on her tides
laid me, unwanted urchin,
in my mother's belly.

My father never forgave me,
as if I had designed the tree myself
and the moon was all my fault, forever
glaring at me with indignant eyes—queue jumper—
pushy bastard even then.
Such small events have made a world for millions:
an afterthought because the telly broke,
the calendar unmarked for want of a pencil.
But I'm lucky—
between a mislaid minute
and Dad for once
with spare change in his pocket—
I came in on a moon and sixpence,
music, stars, and the scent of grass,
and for this, I am grateful.

La Quena Coffeehouse

The singer combs his hair, tosses a coin
before sounding off, spills a prophylactic
of four-letter words, wielding
the act of love
like a club. And he could be right,
for maybe in every coupling, one
wields hegemony, while the other
treads the border
between love and hate.
This wine blurs also the obverse and reverse of the man
intent on reforming the young prostitute.
But Mrs S. knows
Peaches is no spring chicken he can stuff—
on her back, maybe, her legs
up in the air—but no paper frill
around that girl's ankles. Wily bird
she keeps her eye cocked
as he feeds her God and zeal, applauds
the unmusical
musician, guitar protruding
between his legs, the priapus
that can "Fuck America!" maybe,
but never Peaches' mind.

To the Cockroach Fallen in Her Cereal Bowl

Who are you then—Moses Insecta?
Your trip across a wilderness of ceiling
and suddenly
the land of milk and honey arriving—plonk—
under your feet.
How I admire your composure
your instantaneous acceptance
(or rejection)
of miracles!
One thwack and, without pause,
pure as a babe new born
your mandibles bend to the river of milk.
Mr Smith would have taken fever,
written theses, consulted horoscopes,
declared a culture,
made "Dieu et Mon Droit, Mon Droit, Mon Droit"
the national anthem.
But you, with a simplicity
that wipes away the world,
merely stood up to your ankles in the milk
lowered your metallic head
and drank.

Little Lessons

Old Joe's dog has reached its threescore years and ten,
now man wheels pet in a little cart
towards the day of parting. In Crab Park
he tells Mrs S., "He's not ready yet,
he'll see the summer through,"
then falls silent, perhaps seeing
in his dog's blue milky gaze
his own palely approaching hour,
hears within its laboured breath
his own footsteps, slowing.
He points to a spider imposing
its pattern on the world. "We too
can circle, spin a fiction of silver
realizing too late we've bound ourselves
into a corner, that one strong breath
can bring down each bright construct
and that life, when it arrives,
can tear unmendable holes."

Not to be outdone, Mrs S. slurs, "The shea
...'scuse me, *sea*,
matrix where life arose, fern-footed
and shttepped...*stepped*...shorewards
imprinting inshects, animals.
Which was the firsht flower? It had to be white
so that all colours
could deshcend...*descend*...from it, shimple
in form
so that all forms could follow—"
"You're drunk," says Joe.
"No, never, Joe, I promish! Lishen.
No straight line exists—a circle, then—
mirroring life, marked with pointsh...*points*...
to guide us where we're going.

What emerges is shtar-shaped, the white flowers
of Heaven to which the earth turns
for reference. The trick, Joe, my old—my oldest,
dearesht friend—yesh, you are! No, I inshist!—
is to know which shtar…star…is yours, to pin it
in the hair, trusting
as you deshcend…deshcend…*deshend*
the darkness of the stair
that it will lead you
to shweet breezes an' the morning light."
"No, no," Joe says. "Listen
to the treble and bass
of water and sand.
Our ancestral home
was water, and its language
echoes in us. Don't you recognize
primordial myths
in the waves' whispering? What you hear
is an invitation
to re-join Brother and Sister Fish
where they thread silver. Aliens now,
we breathe dust, have humankind
for habitat."
"Why Joe," she says, "You're a philosh—
a philoshopher. Whad's your besht advice
for me?"
"That's easy, Mrs S." says he. "Go sleep it off."

Peaches Talks About Her Mother

Even in her coffin
Mother's face was clenched, as if
she could not let go
while there was yet another bill to pay,
as usual by instalment.
"What did you do, Mother,
when Saint Peter clocked you in?
Did you automatically lift
your pail and brush, begin to scrub
at those pearly gates?
Ah, my mother, my lady
most immaculate, you always had
a double shift, housewife
and cleaning lady, while Dad,
aping all government,
docked a dollar from your housekeeping
for every dollar earned.

So your frown, Mother,
was that a message that Heaven too
is paid for by instalment,
that even in death
there is no rest?
Or was that face a message
for my father, telling him you had
nothing left to give
only your face
clenched
like a fist?"

And Then About Her Father

And sometimes he would torture our dog, clamping
Tecky's muzzle in his big fist, twisting
Tecky's head upside-down
like a black mass, our pet moaning
prayers through its teeth, my sister and I
screaming alongside, his other big hand
holding us off, his giggling crackling
around the room, his eyes coals
beneath charcoal hair, our tears burning
in his smoking breath.

His fingers were brands
on my breasts,
my developing body.
These, and other assaults,
we never forgave.
When he died, only then
did we believe in a merciful God
who answered prayers.

He never spoke of his childhood.
For us, he was only the Great Fire
consuming his daughters
for twenty-odd years. His name
was Tom: our synonym
for hate.

After his death, Mother told me
his red-headed father never called him
by name, only "black bastard"
because of his black hair, and that
when Tom was five, Grandfather rose
from the farm table and silently

flung him into the big kitchen fire,
held up the blazer,* and up Tom roared.

It took six men
to pull Grandfather off. A miracle
you didn't die, they said
when they pulled Tom out, flesh melting,
living torch
in his father's auto-da-fe.

And now I know he never left
that place, and that his soul
revolved endlessly about a stake,
finding no way out through those grown-up faces
and that he never stopped shrieking
his aloneness in those flames,
so he tried to pull
his daughters in.

And now at last I can call you
by your name, oh my father, and let go
my own burning.
When old hatreds kindle,
I shall stand beside you
in your father's fire, hand in hand,
our flesh unravelling, eyes bubbling
in our heads, till our streaming tears
put out our mutual hell.

*A steel shield used to block off the coal fire in order to
encourage a draught.

Gastown

Traffic, a bright sun, the steam clock
gushing the hour. At Mrs S.'s feet
a handful of blue feathers lifts in the wind.
Nothing has changed
except the bird.
The whole of Time gone into that creation, yet
the clock ticks on, the street, the people
are the same, ticking
towards their own transformation
by what claw
to what blue rush of air
while another clock shrieks hourlessly?

Burrard Inlet clashes its symbols of brass
a gull hardens on a rock
its whiteness draining into the wind.
When the tide rises
more than sea-trove is cast up. In Crab Park
Old Joe tells Mrs S., "These seaweeds are bones,
veins of drowned seamen. No longer praying
their voices sigh in the seashells."
Blown back, his words scatter seawards.
Holding high its lone light
a small ship cries out
as it leaves the harbour,
and Old Joe capers, pointing
as the black backbone of the sea
tenses, and drags its long chain…rehearsing, he asks,
whose litany?

On Being Ordered to Cover Her Hair

Dear Vancouver Sun Editor,

Saint Paul is constructing stone by stone
an edifice that will save him
from attacking breasts and buttocks
a high tower erected
against the scent of female flesh.
Women's difference is what gives him nightmares
where breasts float by like water lilies
and a vagina opens with the wantonness
of a summer rose.
"And their hair, brothers, their hair!" he writes
in *1 Corinthians 14:34*
"waterfalls of gold, or a dark warm ocean
for men to drown in
or held back like a red sea
before storming over men's minds!
O brothers, for these sins,
let not the women preach in our churches
where the tides of hair
would wet our dreams, drowning
the holy word!"

Year by year the tower rises,
God made Man in His Image
carved on its cornerstone.
Paul hides in its blunt head, peers
from its lone eye—
Yet even here, the enemy finds him.
Recognizing such a monument, the lilies,
the roses, release their seed into the air
and one has found flesh and taken root, thrusting
up nightly between his thighs.
At last, Paul must take knife

to this thorn
and for this passion and this death
some total twits canonized him.

Very truly yours,

A. Smith (Mrs)

Lest We Forget

"Is it nothing to you?" *asks the stone voice
of the monument. Let us not forget
that in November, politicians
stack against such plinths
their wreaths of pretty poppies, newspeak
for their signatures of blood.
In Victory Square, pigeons cast their vote
against the war memorial, their opinion condensed
into a neat grey minus sign. Loiterers
by choice
they hover near people on benches
whose pride has broken
on the wheel
and deal
that promised jobs.
Only the grass fulfils its promise, courtesy
of sun and rain.

*Inscription carved on the Vancouver War Memorial

Deconsecrated Church

The ball's upward flight
bears prayers through cigarette smoke.
Mrs S. is already on her knees, but
it's some other novitiate who shouts
"Bingo!" a.k.a. "Hallelujah!"

This congregation too
is mostly female and God
is male, bestowing
blessings on both saint
and sinner. Mrs S. mourns
"He never calls my number,"
and from a neighbouring table
comes some poor devil's antiphonal response,
"Lady,
whatever god or gods you got,
He/She/It has got your number all right.
Sooner or later
you'll collect."

Deaf Mute?

(Mrs S. responds to the woman who said,
"What a pity! That disabled couple can never
speak to each other about their love.")

"That dance of fingers
  sheds veils of air, revealing
ten times over
the nakedness of their desire.
Their palms doubly celebrate themselves,
inscribe their love
upon the space between them, enclose
tenderness, shape it
like a flower.
And though the world about them roars
their silence
is their own private universe
wherein they sow a promise: kisses
falling like stars
toward their mouths, each fingertip
a white flame
foreplaying heaven, igniting them
towards that wordless ceremony
where he and she will blaze
in pas-de-deux
and where all language fades
into the profounder silence
that is their bodies, singing."

Pay-Off

Outdoing Cain,
the man bears a cross
carved on both cheeks.
He weighed rent paid, TV repaired
against his friend
and found him wanting, his own wants
butchering the first commandment of this community:
Thou shalt not
inform police or government. Many an eye
hardens on his mouth
from which a tooth
hangs by a thread—bloody tightrope
on which he teeters
between consciousness
and a blessed dark—many an eye
averts, although eventually
Mrs S. the semi-good Samaritan
phones Vancouver General
and like a screaming angel
an ambulance touches down.

Dr Mario

Old Olaf's gone, and Mario the disbarred doctor
inherits his gutter.
He ditched his career
in Howe Street, ripped off
by some snoop from B.C. Med and a woman
he himself defrocked:
pale frond lying
on a charge of patient seduction
(but was not, no—patience be damned—
would not, could not wait
to taste that body.)
He lifts a two-inch weed, a gift thrown
by some god, as she was, as white
as willing to be crushed
as then, as now
and none to see this fierce union
except Mrs S. who will tell all
only to this manuscript,
this paper tiger.

*Mrs S. Finds a Broken Christmas Ornament
During the "Access for the Handicapped" Protest,
Crab Park*

One-winged angel, unearthed from the dust
of this day's protest,
was it by accident you fell
from the celestial city
to huddle like a broken bird
in the Downtown Eastside
where there are no streets paved with gold
and no pearly gates, not even
a wooden gate and railway crossing
for the handicapped?
Were you imitating Christ? Did you try to become
human and poor, and so were maimed
by the doors forever slamming
in your face?
Or maybe you looked down
and were unable to sing
when old men and women
are turfed from their rooms;
when fifty bucks are chopped off
a welfare mother's cheque,
and a ramp, inaccessible and inflated
as a governmental ego,
is built at the intersection
of Big Money and Mendacity.
Or maybe you protested
and when you asked God to intervene
your left wing burned up
and you got thrown out as a trouble-maker
in Paradise...or maybe that fall
from perfection to this
was too much, and it crippled you
to a crooked shadow

plummeting from Heaven, your one wing
screaming.
But maybe the truth
is that you were born imperfect
that you dared ask God for access
and so were banished here, to the Downtown Eastside
where live other damaged angels—
on their backs, shoved out, wings torn off
faces rubbed in the dirt—left-wing angel, welcome home!

Second Service at First United Church

Two hymns down and two to go
while a finger of sunlight
inscribes slow sermons
across the pews, calligraphy of time
to these awaiting the second coming
of free coffee and cookies at eleven.
The priest is nailed
by lack of funding to a cross
he cannot carry, and no Simon
is ever detailed by government. Oh Lord
forgive us our trespasses as we forgive
not the wafer
of welfare, touch lips
with a fingertip of watered wine.
The music goes round and round
and it comes out here
where the water of life
rises to a boil in the kitchen, and there's
one hymn left to go
before Mrs S. (a white-aproned angel)
sings, "Coffee's up," and offers communion
in a plate of Peek Freans, this last
being also love.

Carnegie Centre

Aorta of mahogany and brass
transfusing Chinese, Indians, Whites
towards their own democracy
of cheap coffee and a game of chess.
Here, penalties are not exacted, a smile
is handed back with interest
and a handclasp invests
both grantor and recipient.
In my Father's house
are many mansions: this house
is mansion
to those who spent last night
in Stanley Park
ranting a poetry of rubbing alcohol
and dreaming a room with a gas ring.
Neither light nor warmth
emanates from bureaucracy—it's here
the rootless flora and fauna
of these small streets
draw sustenance,
mounting the steps to this,
their upper room.

Mrs S. Walks Around Her Wine Bottle

A random process of slow turmoil
created an atmosphere
hospitable to life: one small spark
begat this earth. A random process
begat also her consciousness
of that small bottle,
her lonely nights and days evolving
into this. She circles
in slow turmoil, afraid
the bottle is the sun, and she
a small trapped planet
fleeing to the farthest reaches
of her aphelion
only to return, magnetised
by its lucent element—or maybe
she is the moth sucked in
from a long dark
for one last fling with light
although she's well aware
random radiation kills.

Drunk On Main Street

In torn jeans and a crow's feather, Charlie,
(Chief Coyote's son) high-steps out of the pharmacy
his hand a death grasp on some rubbing alcohol.
Aye, there's the rub—
the dream phial that will take him
far from the cold corner of the white man's heart.
His eyes reel, focus on two flies
copulating on dog dirt, high on faeces, dancing
into ecstasy, bum to bum.
He falls to his knees exclaiming
"Hey, at least these fucking flies
have found the fucking secret, eh?
How to extract happiness
from each day's fucking load of shit."

"Come on, Charlie," says Mrs S. "I'll help you home."

"Home? Don't make me puke! Gonna sing
the Skid Row blues…no fucking blue moon croon, only
my blue veins howling
while my brother hacks out tubercular tunes
between pissy sheets.
Fucking back alley blues got me, crazy
beat of trucks and drunks got my mind
pinned and pegged out
in the jingle jangle jungle, cockroaches
dancing till they drop
in my sink, my fucking shoes. No food.
Fucking rats got the best
dumpster treats, leaving sweet
fuck all for me. No fucking money left.
No money, right!
Should I ape my sister, talk fucking monkey talk
to pimps grinning like hyenas

at Main and Hastings?
Pinholes in sister's arms scream fucking blue
murder, scream
fucking cop-car, its blue eye winking at our dark.
Another stabbing, another rape.
Cops got the fucking heat on, pushers
got the fucking heat on, johns
got the fucking heat on, pimps
got the fucking heat on, rage
got the fucking heat on, hate
got the fucking heat on. Mel Tormé's blue moon
never turned to gold,
it fused blood-red!
Know something, Mrs S.?
In the fucking second millennium, torch songs
mean only
another fucking meltdown
in the urban core."

Says Mrs S., "I'll drink to that.
Now hold my arm, Charlie,
and I'll help you home."

Wordbound in the Carnegie Learning Centre

Peaches fidgets
while the rain's transparent flames
bead against the window
the cold sweat of frustration.
The pen is her stake: tied,
she waits for revelation.
Rain casts no shadow, departs
on silence, leaves only
a fading footprint.
The shapes of words
are also secret,
a confused whispering
dissolving the will
of the girl hypnotised
by the drifting, falling tones
on the glass.
This hour
is a grey bubble floating
on a rainy summer
where words swim by, moon-eyed
and meaningless, and comprehension
is a frond drifting
through a drowned memory. Sunrise
and moonrise
will ripple
through all her tomorrows and she
will still be foundering
in a dream of language, clutching
at straws, trying to write
the zig-zagging contours
of words.

Birthday Party on Crab Park Beach

Little Lynn, night-swimming, is a silver fish
confiding to the moonlit inlet
a sort of homesickness.

Budding from Peaches' blood
in that first universe—
that dark sea without stars—
she grew lonely for the moon,
swam out to find a human night,
a moon whose light the sun puts fiercely out.

Then came foster care.

But tonight she swims,
repeating that moment when,
first lifted towards Peaches' heart,
the inaugural glimpse of her bright, wet head
undid the mastery of that strong morning light.

"I didn't want her," Peaches says, "but she came
and something happened
to my heart. Now, I see her
as a new blade of grass
splitting stone."

Ash City (Watching the Film, The Blue Angel*)*

Sharing her TV, Mrs S. tells Rose and Peaches,
"Marlene Dietrich hides somewhere in Paris,
in an apartment without mirrors
and with a big lock on the door.
When the plastic surgeon's knife
fenced with time and lost, this Blue Angel
flew to the hell
reserved for aging beauties (the particularly wounded).
Time's edge whittled Marlene's world
to a fading scrapbook
hidden under a bed in the Champs Elysées.
Life now
is the telephone: umbilical cord
bringing soft semolina, meat
cut in chewable portions,
the day and the night nurse.

Only in dreams
can Marlene run down Hollywood Boulevard
her legs golden blades
mowing down the fans, cutting free
from a City of Lights sinking to ash,
a head on a pillow
its golden fire gone out."

Final Trip

Here's to Mrs Malinowski! The ink
on the six-day sea cruise barely dry,
a hornpipe of exotic place names dancing
on her tongue, and a few salty asides scouring
the frowns of younger relatives, lips pursed
around doubt and disapproval, their scheme
for the nursing home,
the sexless nightie and the carpet slippers,
wrecked on the rocks
of her elderly intransigence.

No barnacles
on that old lady! All such seawrack
left behind, she rollicked up the gangplank
of her own craftiness,
a mickey of bad scotch stuck into her bra,
wearing loud shorts and cheap jewellery that clunked,
bellowing a rude song about sailors and loose women
and planning to blow her pension on bingo.

Mrs Malinowski, leaving on an oceanic sky
and a fleet of stars
with the tide high
and her spirit high
breaking up and out
of outworn flesh and rising
like a lean, clean, silver fish
to seize the dragonfly
of a new morning.

Prostitutes Outside First United Church

The social worker claims incest, says
a cold paternal fire burned them out
before they reached ten years.
Force-fed as baby birds
they are graduates from the fatherly blow job,
plying their trade among the back alleys.

In Grade One they learned their holy grail
is their vagina, communion
is quickie sex, salvation
the hundred-dollar job
when the expense account convention
is in town.

Time is a spider that stores them in a doorway
watching johns bargain
for the twelve-year-olds.
On winter nights
rain leaps like panthers down the gutters,
leaps
like lawyers, judges, police, politicians, pimps,
leaps
like the john with the knife.

Welfare Wednesday

It's Welfare Wednesday, when the fairy godmother
transforms with temporary gold
and Prince Coyote and Peaches
reel down East Hastings
their glass coach a bottle
that will spin them
far from the five-week month
and the mattress under the viaduct
into the Palace of Forgetting
where footmen bow them
into the happy hour
no government can dock, where homelessness
is banished, and theirs is the kingdom
the power and the glory
and Prince and Peaches
live happily ever after, dancing in glass slippers
through the Downtown Eastside.

If wine can flow like water, it will drown
the bawling of the midnight hour,
the glass slippers will not shatter,
Welfare Wednesday not end,
its measure dribbling
to a slop
mopped up
from some plastic bar-room table,
the music not falter, sprawl
into a gutter,
the coach not warp
to paddy wagon
nor the footmen
mutate to rats
scrabbling with them through dumpsters
behind East Hastings grocery stores.

The Abandoned Cat

"I saw him a week ago,"
says the landlady. "I was at the window looking down
and he was underneath, looking up.
He's old, and blind in one eye. Please
don't encourage him."

Mrs S. gazed, and saw herself reflected
in the cat's rheumy eye.

The landlady continues, "Yesterday that cat
placed a rat's head
on the front step
then sat back and waited. His reward
was a bucket of water."

A winter sun hung
its bleached bone, dead leaves
told their beads to the concrete.
That night Mrs S. saw the cat enduring
by a bush, his one eye
a lost star in the moonlight. Already
he was sunken
halfway into earth. Soon, he would be
but a wound in her memory.

Swearing other roomers to secrecy
Mrs S. sneaks him inside,
trawls for donations of fresh milk, canned sardines
and, with luck, *Happy Cat* flea repellent.

Peaches, Rose and Mrs S. Take Tea

Rain comes at them as a wild sea aslant
storming sidewalks and gutters
they tack across,
shoes slurping defeat, hostage
to a dark flux of sky.

Peaches asks,
"What if the sidewalks should open
to this rain's crazy knocking
or we are carried out to sea
by these gutterwise seahorses?"
Rose asks, "What if my high-flying skirt
should balloon us to the Orient,
buffet us hither and thither
on the high tides of these winds?"

Tangled now in umbrellas,
breathless, rain-bloated
mad-haired and giggling,
they are blown into Gassy Jack's café,
signalling weakly
for muffins, scalding tea stiff with sugar
and friendly chairs they anchor to.

Homing

Instinct taking them where they're going
birds are their own hieroglyph
flying close-knit into star or storm.

Without impediments of language
anything may be possible
in a country where Stop
and No Exit and One Way Street
are non-existent and all that flames
is symphony of wing and sun.

Rose and Peaches' hopes
are wing-shaped too,
but they are rooted
in one-hundred-dollar tricks
where the predatory john burns.
They say, close-knit
they might reach star or sun
by such climbing, find their depth,
though such soaring would frighten them
and such unshaping hurt.

Murder is the World's Oldest Profession

In the graveyards of darkened doorways
in the sour back alley slaughterhouses
where night is a black beast
sidling between parked cars,
the johns are waiting, knives cocked
and erect.
Rose had told Mrs S.,
"This red rose is tattooed
on my breast, so that when I'm killed
they'll know who I am."
Now a flat-faced moon balloons
forward, grinning with grey teeth
as the alleys and back lanes
swallow the screams of the disappeared
anonymous women,
their pricelessness pruned
to X dollars per fuck.

Mrs S. weeps,
"The rose tattooed on your breast
was your scream made visual, the tattoo
of death's drum beating
in the darkened car-lot
where that john masturbated blood lust
before consummating with the knife.
Now those careful
to claim they do not know you—
Big Businessmen, judges and politicians—
will play at jigsaw, puzzle
your bloodied anonymity together
piece by piece, while justice haemorrhages
between their fingers.
Polite society does not want
to know you, claims never

to know you, you defile
their image, you remind them too much
of themselves…under the pristine shirt
you are their dirty linen, and your crime
is that you wash it in public.
For this, they will never forgive you,
for this capital offence, they will claim
they have never known
nor will ever know you, will turn
again and again from where you stand
on the corner of your own death.
So what's in a name
but everything: Floozie, Whore, meaning
Disposable Woman, and what was that flower
but a scream
silenced to a stain the colour of blood
on your breast, oh my sacrificed sister,
dead night-flower,
silenced music
of a rose tattoo."

In Memoriam

The blue serge of the sea, ponderous
as a matriarch's hip, heaves
from the canning factory rusting
into history to the totem pole: tower
of childhood cut off
by the father's blade of flesh.

The sea's cadence rises, falls,
like a First Nations accent.
When Mrs S. throws the ashes
and a red rose, she plunges
up to her heart
in the phosphor
of tears.

Mrs S. Talks to the Divorce Lawyer

"When Mr Smith departed from me,
when he withdrew the gift
of himself from me—we lost a child, you know—
it reminded me
of a great storm I saw once
in my home country, when
advancing from behind the far hills
rose an immense curtain: fold
after fold of black cloud
and when all the land was in darkness, the curtain rent
and in the storm's boiling heart
was an unearthly wind, which threw down mighty oaks
and stone walls that for centuries
had been standing. And there was lightning in it,
stabbing, silver fingers
that tore the whole world apart
and left me on my knees
struggling for breath.
Then it passed on like God, too high up
to see what lay wounded
and for long hours afterward the receding light gleamed
with a terrible beauty,
and it was grey, and black shot with gold
and so remote....

So it was with him
and when the storm of him passed, leaving me
parched and barren
as an uprooted tree, I could only crouch
close to earth
for my comfort, and watch him move away
to another country.
And he never looked back, but withdrew
slowly and sombrely

as befits a death.
And in the long years afterwards,
even beyond the far hills
I could still see where he was passing....
It was like another god had come walking
and I too small to matter, so that once again
I was on my knees
with all the breath taken out of me,
except the first storm was shot with gold
and brought rain, while his storm
was all black
and dry as a desert.

Epiphany in Oppenheimer Park

The wind moves in low Gregorian chant
through this white
where trees stand black-robed: configuration
of sin and saintliness.

Snow sighs
from a small branch. It's her child's hand
beckoning to Mrs S.
her child whispering
"This is my peaceful world.
Enter
and be healed."

Ann Jones (ex-Mrs S.) Learns She Has a Brain Tumour

"How slyly you arrived, dark stranger,
how unannounced! First taking up lodgings
inside my brain
and *then* presenting your calling card. Oh, Crabman,
the long years spent tracking me down!
I must have been so difficult to find, so elusive—
British Properties, Downtown Eastside,
society hostess, chicken-killer, shirt seamstress—
how I must have tried your patience, how
many times did you feel like giving up, feel
like going after somebody
less of a chameleon?
But then, in a careless moment,
washing the dishes maybe, or watching TV,
or maybe picking my teeth, my door drifted
open and *wham*—your leg
thrust forward and you were in.

And now, we circle each other, you
with your pincers extended, discovering
I'm not a chameleon, but a Capricornian:
obstinate goat
finding toeholds on air
ever the artful dodger.
Ah, but you consume like a churlish new flame
with your black moods
blowing hot, blowing cold, the hatred
and the love you inspire. But, Crabman, though anxious
for new experiences, I've never
considered bestiality. Also, pity
for you—pity for your malignant grin—
you chose to enter my brain, and the landscape

of my brain is also the universe
of my mind: singular and *infinite*.

Besides, my ex-husband used to say
as a teenager
I was always a Tease
and a Bad Girl. When you pressure me I split
to my private
horizons, laughing.
And though your tentacles spread
and you crawl and crawl
through my veins, searching,
the tunnels of *my* love go on for ever,
and I can hide where you cannot find me,
ever the irritating,
the one who won't be pinned down,
saying one thing, meaning another, agreeing
just for the sake of peace,
then off again, the bad-mannered Capricornian
getting on *your* goat.

And I'd never, ever
give you the satisfaction
of seeing me cry.
But then again, my ex-husband
also said I was Mary Contrary.
One day you might call
and I might just choose to answer,
for the gift you carry between your claws
is a fascination, that beautiful dark sleep
is a temptation and also *my right*.
I never said I envied Methuselah
and you never asked if I wanted to come
just took it for granted I wouldn't
and such machismo annoys me. So one day,
when you have almost given up,

when you're thinking maybe you've bitten off
more than you can chew,
you will call one last time, and I shall answer
in the affirmative
and you'll be *shocked to death*
oh my friend,
my enemy
and my lover."

Acceptance

In Howe Street, the talk
is of tax reform and free trade.
Here among the lesser angels
of unemployment insurance and welfare cut-offs
Ann Jones wanders, her shopping bag
of small talk over her arm. The language
is the corn on her tongue
that stabs with each "Nay Ho Mah?" *
She will never be one of them
yet she is: contradiction
they've grown used to, familiar
in her height and her accent
as a piece of flotsam and jetsam
they now take in stride.
In the grocery store, she speaks
and Chinese sub-titles flash
in their eyes. They hand her
the vanilla bean she didn't know she'd asked for.
For the thirty-third time
she accepts the marriage proposal
of the spaced-out supplicant
at East Hastings and Heatley, and goes home
to tea, to the cat, to the public intimacies
of the lavatory next to her room.
Her landlady exquisitely drafts
her niece's hysterectomy.
It is confirmation, grace
of a sort, and Ann Jones (cat
curled on her knee) stirs it in
with the sugar, with the slow sip
of an afternoon off, with a nod
to the Crabman waiting

* "How are you?"

in the wings. And suddenly
her world is rich
and the first star blooming at her window
is reachable and lovely,
is a branch budding
as the time she has left is,
as these Downtown Eastsiders are
in their singular shining.

ACKNOWLEDGEMENTS

My most grateful thanks to the instructors
at Capilano College and and later at UBC
who introduced me to poetry. Students were
lucky indeed to be taught by such highly
accomplished, dedicated instructors. Many
thanks also for the wisely guiding hand of
Joan Coldwell, my publisher and editor. Finally,
my deepest thanks and admiration go to the
residents of the Downtown Eastside, whose
courage and indomitable community spirit
inspired these pages.

JANCIS MAUREEN ANDREWS was born in Northumbria, England in 1934. At age 14 she ran away from a violent home life and, when apprehended by the police, refused to return to school because she had missed many classes. She was ordered to reform school; later this was altered to one year's probation, which included an order that she not venture outside an area of five square miles. In 1952 she joined the Women's Royal Naval Service and served as a radio operator on the staff of Admiral Lord Louis Mountbatten. In 1965 she immigrated to Canada with her husband, son and daughter. She then took correspondence courses until she had enough credits to study at Capilano College and later at the University of British Columbia where, at the age of 53, she obtained a Bachelor of Fine Arts degree, majoring in Creative Writing.

When her marriage of forty-three years fell apart and her husband refused to pay alimony, Jancis at age 65 took a job as live-in cleaner at a boys' school in England. She returned to Canada after one year and now makes her home in Sechelt, B.C.

Jancis is the author of *Rapunzel, Rapunzel, Let Down Your Hair and Other Stories* (Vancouver: Ronsdale Press, 1992) and *Walking on Water and Other Stories* (Toronto: Cormorant Books, 2009). Her work has been published in numerous periodicals and anthologies and she has won several awards for fiction, non-fiction and poetry. She is an active community volunteer with a particular interest in helping to end violence against women and children. Her personal motto is, "No matter how overwhelming the enemy, you must never give in."